Tadpole Books are published by Jump!, 5357 Penn Avenue South, Minneapolis, MN 55419, www.jumplibrary.com

Copyright ©2024 Jump. International copyright reserved in all countries. No part of this book may be reproduced in any form without written permission from the publisher.

Editor: Jenna Gleisner **Designer:** Emma Almgren-Bersie **Translator:** Annette Granat

Photo Credits: Eric Isselee/Shutterstock, cover; Potapov Alexander/Shutterstock, 1; Dinal Samarasinghe/Alamy, 2tl, 4–5; robertharding/Alamy, 2tr, 3; a_v_d/Shutterstock, 2ml, 12–13; tristan tan/Shutterstock, 2mr, 8–9; ErickPHOTOPRO/Shutterstock, 2bl, 6–7; xijian/iStock, 2br, 10–11; fotolinchen/iStock, 14–15; Hans Harms/iStock, 16.

Library of Congress Cataloging-in-Publication Data is available at www.loc.gov or upon request from the publisher.
ISBN: 979-8-88996-732-3 (hardcover)
ISBN: 979-8-88996-733-0 (paperback)
ISBN: 979-8-88996-734-7 (ebook)

MIS PRIMEROS LIBROS DE ANIMALES

LOS PAVOS REALES

por Natalie Deniston

TABLA DE CONTENIDO

Palabras a saber..........................2

Los pavos reales..........................3

¡Repasemos!.............................16

Índice..................................16

PALABRAS A SABER

alas

ave

cola

cresta

pico

plumas

LOS PAVOS REALES

Veo un ave.

ala

Tiene alas.

Tiene un pico.

cresta

Tiene una cresta.

Tiene plumas.

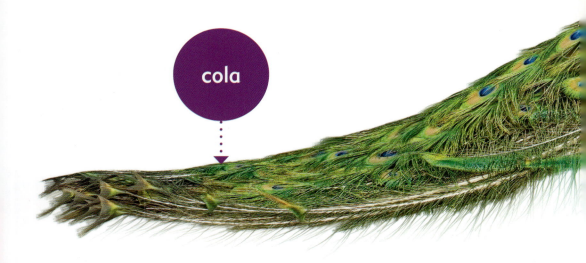

Tiene una cola.

¡Qué bonito!

¡REPASEMOS!

Los pavos reales son aves con muchos colores. Apunta hacia los colores que ves abajo y nómbralos.

ÍNDICE

alas 5
ave 3
cola 13

cresta 9
pico 7
plumas 11